The Tire Kicker

How to Beat the Mind Game & Seize the Results You Want Most

There's something more to life. You know it.

The big question is:

"How do I get more of the results and the life I really want?"

Many find the answer to this question elusive. A few have hacked the answers, and have quickly accelerated to achieving their full potential, and greatest life desires.

Whoever your heroes are, they've had to overcome challenges. They've learned how to operate a mindset of success, and have used the same principles in this book to create extraordinary results. They are still using these principles to maintain their success, and use them to bounce forward to new wins. The beautiful thing is that we can all learn to master achievement. We can enjoy richer finances, more time, better health, enhanced relationships, and greater career and business success, if we apply the same principles.

Here is how to get from simply kicking the tires of life to living your full potential...

Inside These Pages...

Chapter 1: Mind Games   pg. 1

- You've Already Got It
- Winning Is All About...
- Stuck In Reverse
- It's Okay to Have Fear
- The Warrior

Chapter 2: Winning Self-Image   pg. 8

- The Mind Virus
- The Self-Worth Trap
- How To Overcome Self-Doubt
- Creating Good Habits

Chapter 3: Mind Power   pg. 17

- Commitment

Chapter 4: The Magic of Belief   pg. 21

Chapter 5: Action = Power   pg. 23

Chapter 6: Purposeful Planning   pg. 25

- Practicing, Celebrating & Scheduling Success
- Taking Inventory
- Accountability Partners
- Maintaining Good Habits In Good Times
- Daily Success Rituals
- Get Out Of Bed Right

Chapter 7: Jump   pg. 34

Chapter 1

Mind Games

I'm going to help you get unstuck, if you'll let me that is.

I'm so grateful for the space I'm in today. I just celebrated my birthday. It was fun simply hanging out with friends. I also took some time out to reflect on the past, present, and future. There have been some roller coaster moments. And I'm grateful for all of them. I'm on a great life, health, and financial foundation; one that allows me to constantly grow and do more.

Spending time with my sons is one of my favorite things in the world. There isn't anything like it. It's priceless. It can take money, and great lifestyle design to gain this time freedom. But, not everyone I know and meet has that freedom, or joy.

Seeing the same faces, stuck in the same places, with little sign of progress, day after day is tragic. That's what drives me. It's why I invested in creating this book for you.

There is nothing worse than watching someone allow joy, happiness, their potential, and ability to share that with those around them all just slip by. Ever been to one of those cool sushi restaurants where you sit at the bar, and the conveyor belt carries all types of neat and delicious dishes right to you? Life is just like that. Everyone has a favorite or two. Something they've always been curious about trying, or tasting, and sharing with someone special. Yet, some people sit there while those dishes just keep on going by. And another, and another. All you have to do is reach out and touch it.

The world is divided into those that reach out to taste what's being served up, and those that don't, or who are too busy looking at their 'smart' phones to notice their dreams going by.

Let me tell you…anything you want and desire, you can have *if* you reach out and accept it.

You've Already Got It

This is going to burn a little…

You might not feel like you've got what you want right now. The truth is that you do. Now, before you slam this book down, and go back to kicking some more tires, give me a chance to explain.

It's like the first time reading that *"you are earning what you are worth."* Most people think they are worth way more than they are getting paid. Some may have the potential to get paid more. If they step up and take the actions that are worth more.

Yes, life happens. There are millions of things happening in the universe every second that are, and will forever be out of our control. I get it. Yet, none of those things have to stand in our way, if we've got the right mindset and game plan.

Winning is all about beating the mind game.

You might not like what you've got right now. Few people do. The great news is that it can change. Just by taking the right actions now.

There are challenges. We all face the same ones, Yes; me, you, and even Bill Gates and Richard Branson. Recognize that others have already overcome the same challenges we face, and often even greater ones. We can too.

Once we identify the challenges, and the hacks for breaking through them, we can create a profound and highly practical step by step game plan for winning.

It's a lot like chess, we all have the same pieces at the beginning of the game. We may face different challenges, and each bout may require slightly different moves and counter attacks, but if we think, and strategize, and learn winning combinations, we can become champions.

Stuck in Reverse

The biggest challenge plaguing many people is procrastination. Worse than being stalled out on the side of life's highway, the majority of people are stuck in reverse.

The truth is that no business or individual is ever just at rest. Nor can anyone reasonably expect to remain in perfect balance. You are either improving, growing, and moving up, or you are sliding backwards. An eagle may enjoy incredible moments of majestic beauty when it appears to simply float through the air. But if it fails to engage, act, and flap its wings again, it is going to plummet to the ground, and quickly become roadkill for some vulture to devour. Of course, it took some practice and quite a few power moves to get up that high. The immediacy of the situation clearly tells the eagle that it must act to fight gravity. Yet, so many individuals don't feel the urgency in life. Don't ignore gravity. It is real. Even if you can't see it. Even if you can't feel it. Many take the Dory approach to *"just keep swimming, just keep swimming."* Before you know it, they've swum their life away in circles, 'comfortably' numb. You are going to have to battle and conquer indecision, fear, self-worth, commitment, and moving targets to get what you want. But you can do it!

It's Okay to Have Fear

There's no winner that hasn't had to confront fear. For Shark Tank star, Barbara Corcoran, that was fear of failure[1]. For your favorite authors it was the fear of their manuscripts being rejected. For Warren Buffett it was public speaking.

Fear is nothing to be ashamed of. Letting it needlessly control you, and steal your life away is.

What's worse is that most fears are like being afraid of the dark as a child. The fear may be real, but can the dark actually hurt you? How many monsters actually crawled out from under your bed as a child?

---

[1] https://www.entrepreneur.com/video/238230

When it comes to seizing life, and the life you want, you've got to become okay with stepping out of your perceived comfort zone. If you hate eating fruits and vegetables but were marooned on a desert island with only coconuts to survive on, you'd dig in, right? You can choose not to eat or drink them, and starve to death. Or pick up the fruit that nature so kindly dropped right at your feet, survive, and thrive. What are you afraid of? What is more important than that fear?

The Warrior

"Courage, contrary to popular belief, is not the absence of fear. Courage is the wisdom to act in spite of fear." - Peter McWilliams

Nelson Mandela had every excuse to give up, to walk away, and hide in a hole somewhere. If you can think of an excuse, he's probably got you beat – hands down. He had real reasons to fear speaking and action. Yet, Mandela says *"I learned that courage was not the absence of fear, but the triumph over it. The brave man is not he who does not feel afraid, but he who conquers that fear.[2]"*

Put a soldier on a battlefield, or boxer in a ring with Mike Tyson. If they don't have a healthy fear and respect for what a bullet can do to their bodies or a punch in the face from a heavy weight can do to consciousness, they are going to be out of the game in a flash.

---

[2] https://www.goodreads.com/author/quotes/367338.Nelson_Mandela

Winners have a healthy respect for real danger. They know when to cover up. When to tag in a buddy. When to evade. And they know when to strike. After a few bouts, tournaments, and campaigns, they become experts in working through fear and winning. Then it begins to become natural. They know they aren't going to get there unless they make the decision to act, and persevere. That's the difference between those whose names have become famous, and everyone else. You might be surprised at just how quickly your winning instincts can develop in all areas of life. Once you start implementing the right mindset in one or two areas, the results can really snowball.

I usually run to the gym and back early in the morning, at around 4.30 am or 5 am. It's typically still pitch black outside. One morning I was running, and from the dark, I hear the snarling sound of a Pitbull or Rottweiler. I could hear his deep desire to turn me into a snack. Claws were frantically scratching the ground, and although I couldn't see him, I envisioned the owner barely able to hold onto the leash of this beast. As a child, I might have cowered in the fetal position and cried for my parents. But I chose to remain calm and continue on my way. And what happened? Nothing at all. As in the words of immortal Mark Twain, "I've had a lot of worries in my life, most of which never happened." I live by this quote, and don't allow external factors to control my environment.

By making progress, with even the smallest positive actions, we can begin to snowball confidence and adeptness at mastering things we wouldn't have dreamed of before. Once you've gone beyond the basics of providing for the necessities, you can use that to strategize a solution to financial stability, increasing your surplus finances, creating more free time to spend with those you love, and for doing the things you love. Once you've experienced this, it's unlikely you'll be able to hold back from sharing this knowledge and results with others. So kick that tire kicker mindset to the curb. Don't be afraid to start test-driving your dreams. Take action.

Chapter 2
Winning Self-Image

Talking about test driving... how would it make you feel to test drive your dream car? What would it feel like to be gripping the steering wheel of your ultimate dream car? What would the interior smell like? Feel your foot on the gas pedal. How is your posture? Maybe you roll down the windows or drop the top back to share how awesome you are feeling with the world. If you aren't already driving your dream ride, then going out to sit in one is definitely something that should be on the top of your to-do list this weekend. Put it on your calendar now!

True success certainly isn't about money or objects. In fact, I believe that having more money and achieving that type of 'success' is simply a side effect of doing the right things, and having the right mindset. It all flows from mastering the mind game, getting your thinking right, knowing your why, setting goals, and having accountability partners.

Setting aside ego though, having a winning self-image is critical to getting more of what you want. It is the very foundation, or seed that everything else grows from, and is built on. Without it, most gains will be unsustainable.

The Mind Virus

"I got a hustler spirit" – Jay Z (Public Service Announcement)

Poor mindsets sabotage success, good habits, relationships, and cause self-doubt. These negative mindsets result in procrastination and fear of change or of trying new things. I call them 'mind viruses'.

The good news is that The Naked Scientists from the University of Cambridge science podcast[3] remind us that viruses in nature can be good for us too. Think about the vaccines which have saved millions of lives, and have preserved the quality of those lives. On a mental level, books such as this one can be used as positive mind viruses to combat what's bad for you. They can be used to battle against the things impacting your quality of life and holding you back, and what may literally be damaging your health and that of your family. Good ideas and information need to be spread. Not only from person to person as a one shot deal, but as a regular inoculation or dose to keep ourselves from being infected by the bad.

Reading, surrounding yourself with positive people, keeping yourself in a positive environment that will encourage and spur your growth – these are all critical things. It's what winners do. YouTube may be the trendy thing today, but leaders read. Leaders read, collect books, and recommend books to others.

That's why there are billionaires clubs where Buffett, Gates, and Zuckerberg get to hang out, share ideas, and challenge each other. There may be a perceived financial

---

[3] http://www.thenakedscientists.com/HTML/search/

hurdle to accessing these groups. Yet, it's really about the participants wanting to be surrounded with positive minds. They want to be lifted up by bright and minds, not dragged down.

Again, this really isn't about rich or poor, the 99% versus the 1%, educational level, IQ, where you were born, or what title you have at work. Viruses can infect anyone. I can tell you that from firsthand experience. I've been going to national seminars and events almost nonstop for about five years. I've been in business all my life, with at least 17 of those years in real estate. I often get to see the same people again, and again, year after year. It goes something like: *"Hey how are you doing? What are you working on now?"* I typically hear the same answer *"I'm still just learning."* Seriously? There's no progress, no momentum, no action. This plague infects those I know who are highly educated and 'successful' in other careers. They don't know what they want to do, and lack passion. They are victims of their own negative thoughts and self-fulfilling mind virus.

At the same time, we've also seen those resilient to the mind virus, like Oprah Winfrey[4]; those who have transcended every disadvantage and reason not to try. Yet, have shown incredible drive and hustle, and have given back in big ways. The difference is in who you see yourself as, how you feel about yourself, and how you feel about what is possible.

---

[4] http://www.achievement.org/autodoc/page/win0bio-1

> "Success is to be measured not so much by the position that one has reached in life as by the obstacles which he has overcome." – Booker T. Washington

The Self-Worth Trap

> "Shame corrodes the very part of us that believes we are capable of change." – Brene Brown

Author, speaker, and research professor at University of Houston Graduate College of Social Work, Brene Brown delivered an incredibly power packed TED Talk which received over 6 million views online[5]. Her research studies concluded that a negative self-image is one of the most massive and deepest negative forces. It impacts everyone and can be traced to causing all types of atrocious, and self-defeating behavior. Shame or lack of self-worth causes many not to try. They fear the shame of failure. So they just kick the tires, and go back home, instead of pushing ahead.

Know that it doesn't have to go perfectly to be a success, that names don't physically hurt you, and that you don't have to qualify yourself to anyone else to go out there and make your life a success. Period.

It doesn't matter what you've done in the past, what you have failed to do, or what you are afraid of messing up.

---

[5] https://www.ted.com/talks/brene_brown_listening_to_shame/transcript?language=en

Give yourself a chance. Then once you succeed, you may be able to give thousands of others a chance too.

Before reportedly healing many, and becoming one of the bestselling authors of all history, Saint Paul was the raging genocidal murderer of Christians. College dropout Mark Zuckerberg started out with $1,000, made billions, and is now one of our country's most notable philanthropists, pledging to give away around $45B. Sir Richard Branson, who is now considered the most admired entrepreneur in the world by entrepreneurs and CEOs, got his start cold calling and taking pre-orders for music without even having any inventory. What do these people have in common? They all decided at some point not to let their past or present hold them back, and forged ahead to give it their best shot. And the results haven't been too shabby.

"When perfectionism is driving us, shame is riding shotgun and fear is that annoying backseat driver." – Brene Brown

Appreciate yourself for being the amazing miracle you are, be willing just to try, and forge ahead to be all that you can be.

How to Overcome Self-Doubt

"My center is giving way, my right is retreating, situation excellent, I am attacking."

– Ferdinand Foch

How did we become so indecisive?

Indecisiveness and procrastination have become a major problem at every level of life for many. Perhaps you've got a favorite local restaurant. You've probably seen other locals there who know the menu, yet are all tied up in knots over what to order. You can see them physically wrestling with the selections, and incurring a significant amount of real stress. They just can't make up their minds. Often they'll just defer to the same old thing, or abdicate the decision to their waiter. These first world problems are certainly great to have. Sadly, most individuals and families end up treating their finances, investments, and futures the very same way. Blame it on the noise, too many choices, or lack of time; but it really means giving someone else control of your daily life and future. You've got to make decisions based on your gut and roll with them. Fortune favors the bold.

We must stop second guessing ourselves, and start pushing forward. That starts with recognizing that indecision and procrastination are among the biggest threats to our success. Don't let them beat you. Attack these detractors head on. Some people are naturally more comfortable with making decisions than others. If that's not your strong suit, then take a page out of Warren Buffett's playbook. In a Forbes report on how Warren Buffett and Joel Osteen conquered their fear of public speaking; Buffett chose to enroll in a course to help him gain the courage to speak publicly[6] and Osteen just got up and preached week

---

[6] http://www.forbes.com/sites/carminegallo/2013/05/16/how-warren-buffett-and-joel-osteen-conquered-their-terrifying-fear-of-public-speaking/

after week. So learn what you can, and do what you fear – often, and it will become easy while making you better at it.

How we perceive things makes all the difference in what we can accomplish, are willing to try, and how easy it comes. It's not about unrealistic optimism or putting the blinders on. The data shows our chances of survival when wearing a seatbelt are a lot better. So I wear a seatbelt. I don't run through traffic with my eyes closed just hoping my positive attitude will prevent me from getting squashed. I've learned that crossing even the busiest roads is easy if you find one of those pedestrian crossings and act on the green light.

But there is always another way to look at things or another way to get it done. One of the most powerful analogies you can ever master is knowing that it doesn't even matter if the glass is half full, or half empty. Not if you can pick up a pitcher or a hose, or turn on a faucet and fill it up whenever you like. One of my team members calls me an 'inverse paranoid.' I had to look that up the first time I heard it. It means that I am always looking at challenges in a positive way. I don't ignore the fact that real challenges are happening. I ask *"How can this benefit me? How **will** it benefit me?"*

Creating Good Habits

"Successful people are simply those with good habits." – Brian Tracy

Creating good new habits is the path to success in whatever you want. We are our habits. Fortunately, we all have the power to change them.

If your habits are to eat terrible food and sit on the sofa watching TV every day for ten years, there would certainly be a noticeable difference in your physique compared to if you ate well and exercised every day. When it comes to good health and fitness, there are no shortcuts. But you can decide your future by beginning to create the habits that will turn you into the winner and image you desire. You don't even have to start worrying about giving up anything at this point. Start by asking what small things you can do every day to get where you want to go. It could begin with drinking an extra couple glasses of water or taking the stairs instead of the elevator. Then build on that.

The same goes for relationships. If you want to have a great, strong relationship in ten years, you start finding ways to do little things to build that each and every day. In contrast; if you allow yourself to be lazy and irritate your spouse every day for the next ten years – guess what kind of relationship you'll have then?

Finances are no different. Everyone wants to get rich overnight. Dangerous short cuts in this area often have the same effects as crash dieting or creeping over the fence to see if the grass is greener when in a relationship. Make smart financial choices every day, spend a little better, save a little, invest a little, demand slightly better returns, and before you know it you can be in the financial situation you had been dreaming of.

The easiest way to understand this is looking at children. What you pour into them, teach them, and have them do each day molds them into the person they become when they are ten, a teen, an adult, and even as grandparents.

Lao-Tzu said, *"A journey of a thousand miles begins with a single step."* Imagine if Gandhi or Martin Luther King Jr. had never taken the first steps on their marches. Amazing and massive change is possible with just a little action. Sometimes it is as simple as a step. Sometimes that first step is made alone, but before you know it you've got a movement.

Envision the life you want. Know your why. Know what your ultimate life looks and feels like. Then start adding small positive habits into your daily routine. A glass of water, a carrot, a five minute walk, cooking dinner for your spouse tonight, spending 15 minutes of quality time with your kids tomorrow, picking up a new book to read after this one, or requesting more information about an investment you've been thinking about – these are all great ways to start on the march to massive change in your life.

Chapter 3
Mind Power

Our minds are still far more powerful than computers. Even using a tiny fraction of their capacity we can create amazing change. Unfortunately, many have yet to champion the first of the three building blocks to unlocking their potential. If you are ready to change that, here is how to master that in three steps...

Commitment

"The biggest commitment you must keep is your commitment to yourself" – Neale Donald Walsch

Commitment is the foundation of true and sustainable success of all types. If you can't commit to yourself, how can you commit to anything? That includes relationships, family, starting a business, a financial plan, anything. If you can commit to yourself, you can commit to anything.

Almost invariably, the winners are simply those that can commit to staying in the game longer. In the words of Babe Ruth, *"It's hard to beat a person who never gives up."* That's true of companies, startups, investments, running, boxing, baseball, battle, marriage, and surviving trying times in your personal life. Look at Mohammed Ali and others who managed to win and become champions because they stayed in the ring and wouldn't give up.

Make promises to yourself. Find the path. Push forward, and grow. The statistics on new gym memberships, and ensuing drop out rates after the New Year, each year, are staggering. The same goes for diets and products for quitting smoking also. I'm not asking you to change your whole life tomorrow. I'm not asking you to change anything for me. I do want you to experience the best life you possibly can, and to experience your full potential. Add great new things into your life each day. Thoughts, good habits, and actions which will carry you to the goals you have committed yourself to.

There are several practical tools and strategies which can really help with commitment:

1. Written goals
2. Reviewing your goals daily
3. Accountability partners
4. Spending more time in conducive environments
5. Adopting systems

If you haven't yet - write your commitments down, right now. What are the top 3 to 5 things you are committed to? Make these a sticky note, a screensaver, or a poster and read them twice a day. Especially first thing in the morning. You'll also find special pages at the back of this book to help you get clarity on this.

Having a positive environment and surrounding yourself with people that will help you grow is incredibly powerful. Who you know (and who knows you) is still often more powerful than what you know. The universe can give you an incredible hand up to where you want to be if you put yourself in the right place and around the right people.

You won't always get this right the first time, and people change. Perhaps you've been ditched by a gym buddy because you were holding them back and couldn't keep up. Maybe you've already tried to break some bad habits, and you've realized that it also required not hanging around the same old people. Maybe this has shown up in your personal relationships too. I am no different. When I look at myself in terms of commitment, I see some issues regarding companions. Sometimes it doesn't work out. Things change. If there is symmetrical growth and change in both parties, it can work. You can keep building each other up to higher levels together. If only one of you is growing and the other is declining or remaining stagnant, then there is usually trouble. Maybe you have felt someone is holding you back, or have been ditched by a partner because they felt you were holding them back in the past. You need to be around individuals who are helping you continuously grow.

Birds of a feather flock together. That applies to sports teams, personal fitness, business success, and investments. Groups of fit people weren't born that way, nor were they born close friends. If you want to be physically fit, hang out with fit people. Learn from them and adopt their healthy habits and systems. If you want to be financially fit, hang out with those who are successful, learn their habits, and adopt their systems. Research by the founders of Little Pink Houses of America, published in Realty411 Magazine, shows that you are at least 4-6x more likely to be successful in reaching your goals if you adopt a system and have a support network, versus just having the information and trying to work on it alone[7].

Each person reading this will have a unique personality and perception, will be at a different point in their lives, and will find slightly different tactics work best for them. You may be at a place in life where you just want to build a strong foundation to launch from. That's great. Just don't settle. Keep stretching. Or perhaps you are in a position where you are ready or need to make a big leap forward, or just to distance yourself from that junk back there. For the first group, taking solid, consistent steps is a great strategy. If you are ready for the leap though, put yourself in a position where you can only move forward. Think about mountain climbers. They get up there. They really commit to climbing that wall. Often the only way is up. Sometimes there may not be a visible path that is easy all the way to the top. They manage to figure it out one finger and foothold at a time. You can too. Alexander the Great is credited with the order to "burn the boats." Arriving in enemy territory, and despite being incredibly outnumbered, he instructed his army to burn their ships. After that, they simply had to succeed. There was no turning back, no retreat. They had to figure out a way forward, and a way to conquer as they had committed to do.

---

[7] http://realty411magazine.com/tag/little-pink-houses-of-america/

Chapter 4
The Magic of Belief

"Those who don't believe in magic will never find it." –
Roald Dahl

You attract what you think about and focus on. You get what you believe in. The beautiful thing is that we get to choose what our beliefs are, which are fueled by desire - many thought leaders and highly successful investors and real estate CEOs credit their success to having said "burning desire. They say it is what differentiates their successful prodigies from the 99%. It is quite easy to burn with desire and bright ideas, for a moment. Most fade out, though. To make the magic happen, and see it through to the really big miracles happening, you have to believe. You have to have faith in that belief.

Faith and belief are a choice. They are a choice beyond what you can see. They are not based on what you are tempted to feel. First, you believe in the possibility. Then you see it realized. It is scientifically proven that things tend to be as hard or easy as you perceive them. If you believe it is impossible or you are doomed, guess what you get? On the other hand, incredible achievements have happened simply out of having a more optimistic perspective, and believing they could happen. Elon Musk and his Tesla, SolarCity, and SpaceX ventures are great examples of this.

I remember when the world collapsed from the economic crises of 2008. I remember just laying on my back. I didn't know what to do. For a moment all seemed lost. I had no idea what direction to go in. I lacked the energy to move. Then I decided to refuse to give up. I grabbed on to the desire to make the best of the situation. I nurtured and developed the feeling, and fueled that spark and flame into burning desire. Then from desire to belief it was possible to create new success. I began visualizing what the future could look like. Then set concrete goals and an action plan.

Positivity, belief, and a good plan don't mean you'll be magically transported to your desires without any traffic, detours, or the need to refuel and service the engine a little. But if you cling to your faith and belief during those moments, you will make it. You will find the path, and you'll make it.

Chapter 5
Action = Power

Understanding that action is power is the third building block of success.

The 3 Pillars of Success:

1. Commitment
2. Belief
3. Action

Some say knowledge is power. That's not true. Take a martial artist for example. Strength, speed, knowledge of technique, and action are all separate qualities. Muscle means nothing without speed and technique. Speed is nothing without technique or strength. Neither knowledge nor strength have any significance unless they are put into action. It is then that they become power. They become a force.

What if Babe Ruth never swung the bat?

What if Mohammed Ali never stepped in a ring?

What if Steve Jobs never made that pitch?

It's worth taking a moment to really appreciate the importance and value of action.

Assign the full amount of relevance and value to action that it deserves. Everything you want is on the other side of that action. You aren't ever going to feel it, taste it, experience it, or enjoy it unless you take that action.

The Tire Kicker

Virtually every moment spent kicking the tires is lost time that you'll never get back. So get in and test drive it. Seize your future by taking action, and enjoy it. Or resign yourself to whatever you have now, and how much that will degrade over time if you don't move forward. Just keep wasting time kicking tires.

Chapter 6
Purposeful Planning

"Wake Up Determined. Go To Bed Satisfied."

– Dwayne Johnson (The Rock)

So how do you start taking action and begin building positive momentum?

1. Know yourself
2. Harness the mindset that will allow and drive you to take action
3. Excitedly take on new things, looking forward to overcoming challenges
4. Practice saying "Yes" and taking action
5. Put the right framework into place to propel your action
6. Just do it!
7. Have a system to maintain your momentum and results

Some of you may be saying "well, it's easier said than done." Which may be true for those that have spent years practicing procrastination, and brainwashing themselves into thinking they are simply procrastinators. Those are lies of the "lizard brain" the most primitive part of our human brain. You can put practical elements into play to drive yourself forward.

Practicing, Celebrating & Scheduling Success

Start by knowing yourself. Know what makes you tick, what makes you stall, and what makes you leap forward. Look at your calendar and identify the detractors that may attempt to sabotage you. Avoid them. Then put in those things which will pull you upwards. Start by celebrating in advance.

Celebrate tonight knowing that life is about to change. Go out and celebrate because all the things you want are coming. Take your partner out to dinner, take your son or daughter out for a giant ice cream sundae, go buy a round of coffees for the locals in your favorite joint, or even get on Skype or Google Hangouts and have a virtual video celebration with a faraway friend or sibling. Awesome things are coming.

Now set up rewards for yourself as you reach each milestone on your journey. Set up a reward system to pull you forward through each action you need to take. That might be a steak dinner if you clear all the calls on your list tomorrow. It may be a fabulous honeymoon after you propose. It could be indulging in your favorite pizza after making a tough pitch. Or it could be setting a date to buy your dream car after you have invested in real estate for 6 to 12 months. Give yourself drivers, and they'll pull you through faster than you thought.

If you have massive dreams, and you don't even know all the steps to get there yet (which should be the case), then begin small by practicing saying yes, and taking small steps each day. Say "Yes" to every opportunity you can.

Will you donate that extra dollar to charity when buying your groceries? "Yes." Will you meet up for coffee or dinner or that kids' playdate? "Yes." Will you invest a small amount in that new mortgage note fund you just got the email about? "Yes!" Then reward yourself after each yes.

If you don't know all the steps or have been making excuses to keep kicking tires because you just don't know all the information – then make today the day you it find out.

There are few excuses for kicking tires today. With the internet you can find out anything about that vehicle you've been wanting from your phone in under five minutes. Get the Carfax, Google the reviews on the make and year, and check out the online reviews of the dealer. Or if you are looking into a new career or investment – sign up for that course or sign up for the email newsletter or blog feed of a couple of websites and start getting fed that information every day. Maybe even buy a book to read after you finish this one.

Make a list of all the actions you need to take to get to your goals. Break them down as small as you need to, and put them on your calendar. One for each day. Every day do that item first. Before you know it you will have made incredible progress.

Once you begin snowballing success, it will come easier and easier, and so will taking new actions that propel you to even greater heights.

Taking Inventory

Why do some people achieve such great success and then burn out? Why do some soar and then crash? All while others seem to stay at the top of the game? We see this in the music industry, acting, sports, real estate, and the financial world. Most often it is a result of losing focus on what's most important, as well as getting lost on detours that don't end up where you really wanted to go. I discovered this the hard way. Then I found an excellent way to prevent it. I want you to not only get what you want and experience the joy that comes with taking action but to keep up that momentum too.

I now regularly take inventory of where I am, what I have been achieving, and the direction I've been going in. I do this every six months. I track my progress against my goals to see how I am performing in each area and then identify where I may need to raise the bar and set higher goals, as well as where I may need to apply more focus to catch up. For example; if you've been checking off all of your buying goals, but not your time and net worth goals – that's a problem waiting to happen. Having three brand new Benz in the driveway, but working 100 hours a week just to shell out $70,000 a month in bills isn't sustainable.

Taking inventory may just mean a couple of hours at night over a cup of tea, or better yet – a regular retreat where you get away to think for a couple of days. It can be on the anniversary of reading this book, New Year's Eve, on your birthday, or any other day that works. Just schedule it in way ahead of time. Take a moment to set that up on your calendar now.

Accountability Partners

Accountability partners are one of the most powerful tools you'll discover and put into play. The perfect example of this is, if getting in shape is one of your goals you might hire a personal trainer. You pay for that trainer's appointments, those scheduled workouts and their expertise. That side-by-side motivation and accountability help you show up, do the work even when you don't feel like it, and push yourself to hit your goals. There is no question that you will do more, and see better results with a fantastic coach. You can use accountability partners in every area of life from spirituality, health and fitness, career and finances to relationships, and everything in between.

There are many ways to leverage accountability partners. Some are free and some may require a substantial investment. I have personally learned to invest big in this area.

Some of these options may include:

- Friends and family
- Business coaches
- Professional advisors
- Meetup groups
- Boards of directors
- Trainers and educators
- Your peers

Learn from, leverage, and be propelled by these partners. 'Shadowbox' with them if need be, until it becomes natural, and you are ready to get in the real ring. The more you surround and keep yourself around good people and in good energy environments, the more you will thrive. This is exactly why Silicon Valley exists and continues to be a magnet for aspiring entrepreneurs, regardless of the fact that housing there is so insanely expensive.

Maintaining Good Habits in Good Times

What we do in good times and at our peaks is just as, if not more important than what we do when we are experiencing dips, or are just starting out. It's what we do at the top which has the power to topple us and throw us down a lot harder than we anticipate. This is especially true when things like the economy and industries change. All too often ego takes over and we start to forget what was really propping up our success. We think we've made it, and we stop doing those things which really got us to the top. It doesn't take long for new bad habits to sabotage everything that was built and gained.

Commit now to maintaining good habits. They'll see you through.

Five of these are:

1. Documenting everything you do – i.e. journaling
2. Celebrating and anchoring great moments and milestones
3. Purposefully creating a positive mental map and timeline

4. Always creating an advanced schedule for learning and setting new goals
5. Creating a plan to ensure continuity and protecting your gains as you grow

These habits will help you avoid the worst when others are facing challenges, will keep you on track, and if you do slip they'll make it 1,000 times easier to bounce back even higher and faster.

Daily Success Rituals

Success rarely comes overnight. Rather, it is the culmination of a series of small steps, and their maintenance. It is through daily habits and rituals that a lifestyle is designed, created, and success is achieved.

So what are some of the rituals which can help you operate at your best and achieve what you want? What do those you aspire to be like do on a daily and weekly basis, which keep them moving at peak performance? This is an absolutely individual area where what works for someone else may not work for you. The diet or exercise regimen or sleeping schedule of one person may not produce the same results for someone else. But you will find common characteristics and habits among the successful.

Some of these are:

- Reading
- Using positive language
- Meditation
- Exercise

- Journaling

These habits don't happen on their own. Just like by not having a birthday marked on your calendar, you are more likely to forget it. Or if you only have junk food in the fridge you are likely to eat unhealthily – growing positive habits, like the ones mentioned, takes preparation, planning, and a bit of discipline.

Some ways to fuel the above are to go out and buy a handful of books to keep stocked up on, signing up for an online course, using an app to get new words every day and consciously using more positive words daily, paying for a gym membership or yoga classes so that you go, and buying a great journal and setting up an attractive nook in your home to work on it every morning or night.

Get Out of Bed Right

All the best intentions for today and tomorrow may just be wishful thinking unless you get up, and get up right.

Live a life that has you jumping out of bed with purpose. Wake up with a sense of urgency to take action. If that doesn't describe your mornings, then something isn't right. It's true that this morning rush might not come very naturally to everyone, but it is achievable and makes life so much better. To get there, you might either have to change the direction of your life or just put the right structure into play to facilitate that.

You don't have to change your life overnight to go from dreading crawling out from under the covers and putting your feet on the floor, to actually enjoying getting up. All you need is belief and a dream to work towards. Look forward to the actions you can take to get there tomorrow morning, and each morning. That's the mindset that will get you charged and energized every morning.

There are plenty of ways to amplify your mornings and how you wake up to facilitate this feeling of aliveness. It may be as simple as a better alarm tone. It could be eating a healthier breakfast to get you energized. It may be scheduling something you really love first thing every morning. Or perhaps it will take installing a visual call to action above your bed, on your nightstand, or on the wall in front of you. Get a custom piece if you can. "Carpe Diem!" or "Do Something Awesome Today!" Both will work just fine too.

Decide in advance that this will be a great day. Commit to making it a successful day. And go make it happen!

Chapter 7

Jump

"Soon is not as good as NOW." - Seth Godin

You know what you want. You can have it.

If you put the principles in this book into play, you can start making great leaps toward the life you really want.

Everything you want is just on the other side of taking action. Own that dream, see it, get the awareness and mindset you need to set yourself on the path to sustainable success, put the right framework in place, and commit to it.

Now Go Do It!

"If it's both terrifying and amazing then you should definitely pursue it."

You CAN Do This! I Believe In YOU!

If you'd allow me, I'd love to help you on your way...

Additional Resources & Further Reading

Love this book? Dig in and get more like this from these books…

Turning Distress into Success – Fuquan Bilal

It's Your Turn – Seth Godin

Before Happiness – Shawn Achor

Extreme Ownership – Jocko Willink

Breaking into the Light – Maria Garcia

Think & Grow Rich – Napoleon Hill

Special Thanks

Special thanks to:

My sons who inspire me to do it all.

My editor Maria who helped make this readable.

My mentors and accountability partners who kept me on track to completing my second book.

Read It & Share It

If you care about someone, give them a copy of this book. Use the following spaces to enter the name and date you dedicate it to someone new. Keep passing it on and see what you create by sharing the power of this information...

If this is your personal copy and you've got extra to share, use this space to record each time you read or come back to this book as a journal for later on...

Action Section:

Use this section to begin to put this book into play and take the power steps to seizing the life you really want most.

What is it that you really want most?

I want:

1. _____

2. _____

3. _____

What are some practical steps to take that will make you feel better about your self-image?

1. _____

2. _____

3. _____

4. _____

5. _____

The Tire Kicker

Name 5 things you are good at, or have accomplished in the past:

1. _____
2. _____
3. _____
4. _____
5. _____

Name 3 people who have overcome bigger obstacles than you face, or who have achieved the type of life you want:

1. _____
2. _____
3. _____

Good habits that I can start today:

1. _____
2. _____
3. _____

I am committed to:

1. _____

5 people that might make good accountability partners:

1. _____

2. _____

3. _____

4. _____

5. _____

5 places I can find more accountability partners:

1. _____

2. _____

3. _____

4. _____

5. _____

I am going to celebrate my coming success this week by:

_____

One action I can take today to begin getting more of what I want is:

_____